Q & A

Q & A

ADRIENNE GRUBER

BOOK*HUG PRESS 2019

The production of this book was made possible through the generous assistance of the Canada Council for the Arts and the Ontario Arts Council. Book*hug Press also acknowledges the support of the Government of Canada through the Canada Book Fund and the Government of Ontario through the Ontario Book Publishing Tax Credit and the Ontario Book Fund.

 Canada Council **Conseil des Arts**
for the Arts **du Canada**

Funded by the Government of Canada   Financé par le gouvernement du Canada    Canada

ONTARIO ARTS COUNCIL
CONSEIL DES ARTS DE L'ONTARIO
an Ontario government agency
un organisme du gouvernement de l'Ontario

Book*hug Press acknowledges the land on which it operates. For thousands of years it has been the traditional land of the Huron-Wendat, the Seneca, and most recently, the Mississaugas of the Credit River. Today, this meeting place is still the home to many Indigenous people from across Turtle Island, and we are grateful to have the opportunity to work on this land.

Library and Archives Canada Cataloguing in Publication

Title: Q & A / Adrienne Gruber.

Other titles: Q and A

Names: Gruber, Adrienne, 1980- author.

Description: Poems.

Identifiers: Canadiana (print) 2019006482X | Canadiana (ebook) 20190064838 | ISBN 9781771664721 (softcover) | ISBN 9781771664738 (HTML) | ISBN 9781771664745 (PDF) | ISBN 9781771664752 (Kindle)

Classification: LCC PS8613.R79 Q2 2019 | DDC C811/.6—dc23

PRINTED IN CANADA

For Quintana Roo Elizabeth Gruber-Hill

CONTENTS

QUESTIONS

We split a self in such a way that there isn't enough
for either of us.

The first lesson of motherhood:
pretend you are brave until
you are brave.

Fact: death too is in the egg.

Try to remember
the seductive sea if you can.

For each night is a long drink
in a short glass and birth is
but a sleep and a forgetting.

Fact: the body is dumb, the body is meat.

I had no force left in me
but a voice in my head:

to have a child is to give
fate a hostage.

Once she was born
I was never not afraid.

Q: Here, put this baby in your shirt.

A: I really don't feel like being pregnant with your doll right now.

Q: Just do it. Then I'll give you sips of water until you give birth.

A: Okay, I guess.

Q: That's it, drink the water. Oh look, the baby's out.

A: That was easy.

NOT TRYING

We made love before his stitches came out.

We came before his wounds had time to heal, before his cells multiplied and layered and stitched together, before the tiny rivets in his torso dried up, before he could bend and contort, before flesh was remade flesh.

We joined and twinned and twinned again, sinking into each other, boots into wet earth.

We smeared a salty rub in rock, spun tales and drew pictures on cliffs that our waves crashed against.

We bore claws and teeth.

We made spit pacts and blood oaths and pinky swears.

We moulded casts of our genitals to show our children, moistened riverbanks until the red earth grew shadows and it poured.

We promised it wouldn't hurt if we held still.

We unmade the bed against the surgeon's advice.

We made sure he could still heal—the waves, unless there is weather, are calm, roll a body gently.

We unmade dirty deeds and made them dirty again.

OVULATORY LINEAGE

Like Matryoshka dolls
we incubate. Mom and I,
1948.

WHAT TO EXPECT WHEN YOU'RE EXPECTING (100 YEARS AGO)

Longings

We do not approve of the common practice
of humouring her every whim and fancy.

Mustard, pepper, hot sauces, spices will engender
a love for stimulants in the infant.

The use of flesh food is to be condemned as harmful
to the digestion or interests of the child.

Excessive use of tea and coffee stamp the progeny
with vicious tendencies and even fatal disease.

Self-denial, the subordination of desire and convenience,
must result in good to the mother and the child.

Those in whom longings are the most imperious are those
of an impulsive disposition and without self-control.

Exercise

Washerwomen work up to the day of confinement,
then resume their occupation the next day.

The exercise afforded by household duties
constitutes the best conditioning of the trunk and limbs.

If on a journey, an Indian woman will deliver her child, then
promptly mount her pony and proceed to her destination.

When long walks cannot be taken,
carriage riding may be substituted.

The ease with which the Negro women of the South
give birth has long been remarked upon.

High-class women maintain high-class idleness.
Bad bodily conditions arise from indolence.

A lazy woman bears a long,
painful childbirth.

Bathing

Have no fear that the bath will disturb
the contents of the womb.

Special attention must be given to local cleanliness.
Increased blood supply of female parts increases localized secretions.

The best means for flushing is the siphon or fountain syringe.
For further directions, see appendix.

A little soap should be used. If there is an abundance of leucorrhea,
consider special remedies.

These baths are the most valuable additional means
of facilitating the exit of the infant.

The temperature should not deviate from that of the body.
A hot or a cold douche might occasion a miscarriage.

Indulgence results in the transmission of libidinous
tendencies to the child.

It is a well-established fact that the propensity
to abortion is induced by sexual appetite.

The practice of continence during pregnancy
is enforced in the harems of the East.

Abortion is practised among women who desire
to remain special favourites of the common husband.

Continence during gestation ensures the pains
of childbirth are greatly mitigated.

A woman's sexual nature should find expression in motherhood,
not the grosser forms of sexual activity.

The females of most animals resist advances of the males
during this period. They are less perverted than humans.

Influence

Every Breeder knows that disease
and vicious tendencies are transmissible.

Moral as well as mental qualities are passed down,
which we know from the criminal class.

If a man expends a thousand dollars for a fine horse,
he inquires with great care into the ancestry of the animal.

Family susceptibility to scrofula, consumption, insanity, or epilepsy
should be considered by a young man seeking a wife.

The habit or vice of the parent becomes an
irresistible urge in the offspring.

A state of anxiety long maintained during pregnancy
produces idiocy in the child.

PLAYA DEL CARMEN, QUINTANA ROO

Ten days after our wedding we recline
at El Fogon, swill cocktails with four shots
of tequila. Our food comes and we're brined—
Dennis performs looping gestures, parrots
his drunk sperm. We stagger to the hotel,
pass out on towel swans entwined. Hijacked
with headaches, our dehydrated tongues swell.
Fuck tipsy and frenetic, the odds stacked
in our favour—I'm ovulating. Dazed,
we fly across three countries, bodies sour.
At the Houston airport, an egg, unfazed,
lobs along my Fallopian tube. Hours
pass as a slightly headachy sperm fights,
swims forward with all its hungover might.

MOTHER FAILURE BEGINS IN UTERO

As many as eight
million eggs mass in fetal
ovaries. Dying.

HYGIENE OF ANTENATAL LIFE

A child born as the result of a union in which both parents were in a state of
beastly intoxication was idiotic.
> —J. H. Kellogg, *Ladies' Guide in Health and Disease: Girlhood,*
> *Maidenhood, Wifehood, Motherhood,* 1902

The special influence of the mother
begins at conception.

Mothers transmit piety to their children in larger measure
than fathers by a proportion of nearly three to one.

Anger, envy, irritability of temper
should be held in check.

She should cultivate cheerfulness of mind, calmness of temper,
and avoid excitement of all kinds, such as theatrical performances.

Her husband must encourage her to resist such tendencies
through interesting conversation, reading, and various harmless diversions.

Mothers are as likely to transmit their enfeebled mental qualities
to their sons as to their daughters.

Stock raisers appreciate that blood has market value
and don't ruin animals by allowing them to propagate freely.

The haphazard way in which we generate humans
leaves no room for surprise that the race should deteriorate.

GESTATIONAL FALL

You must harden yourself to a lot of hard, uncomfortable and difficult hiking. That's both the expected and unexpected requirement of the West Coast Trail. It's tough, everyone knows that. But it's tough in a way that expectations realize and don't understand. It's wet. Wet all the time. Wet in a way that saps enthusiasm. Tires you quickly. Makes you rush, slip on stairs, jump onto a wet rock that will break your leg… This is the thing you must brace yourself for…you have to have true grit.

—West Coast Trail Guide

I slip on a wet ridge and 35 pounds of pack pull my body down. The forest is a dazzle of green and brown, light and dark. The rock face barbs my hands, sloppy and useless, the rock face, sawtoothed and serrated, my hands, desperate.

v

On departure day our boat left at 6 a.m. and we were the only people on the ocean. We bundled in greasy wool blankets and watched California Greys breech, vapour exploding like bullets from blowholes. Docked at Bamfield—eggs Benny and a hotcake each—and hitched a ride to the trailhead.

v

I slide and tumble, abrading rock with my own skin. The earth spins. I am the axis.

∨

We planned this trip before you were conceived. At my
first prenatal appointment, my doctor discouraged us. Said
I shouldn't carry more than 10 to 15 pounds. I quickly grew
accustomed to my 35-pound pack. Why hadn't I brought more
food? I was starved. I snuck M&M's from everyone's trail mix.

∨

I'm going to die three kilometres from the boat that will take
us home. It was naive of me to think we would get out of this
unscathed.

∨

Early on, my nausea ceased. I felt strong. Tide pools were open
eyes. In them, I saw our future. My skin became a salt lick. I
began to dream. Please have your father's fierce eyes, his warm
slow voice.

∨

I think about you. My selfishness. I wanted to prove we could
exist as whole beings, simultaneously. In spite of you. Because.

∨

Boots etched the sand. When we turned to look at how far we'd
come, our shuffled steps were sluiced. The trail was eager to be
rid of us. Once inland we marched like soldiers.

v

My pack protects my head and neck from bashing against rocks, but it also disturbs my equilibrium, prevents me from finding my grip on the jutting rock face or stopping myself with a tree branch. It adds weight to my fall.

v

According to Google, a woman in late term hiked the trail but didn't know she was pregnant. Coast guard evacuated her via floater suit against 1.5-metre swells. She assumed appendix or spleen. Thirteen hours later, a seven-pound girl was in her arms. The fetus she thought she lost eight months earlier, the baby's twin.

v

There is nothing between you and me and this ridge that doesn't give a shit about us.

v

We bathed battered limbs, soaped sour from armpits, between thighs. The sun mauled our shoulders. Sweat pooled under my aching breasts. It hurt to speak in full sentences, so we puffed out words, mostly *fuck* and *cock*.

v

There is a drop coming. If I don't stop myself now, I never will. One more pull of my pack, gravity and its properties, and you and I have very different futures ahead of us.

v

When we registered at the trailhead, the whiteboard in the office read: *Total Evacuations To Date: 53.*

v

Neither of us knows our future.

v

The boardwalk was a collection of trees' bones, staggered and skewed. When we stopped to refuel, our packs loomed like monsters against trees. The trail made sure my hunger was bottomless.

v

I can't stop or save us. We're nearly over the edge of the 30-metre drop, a pit where 100-year-old trees are ready to skewer us. My hands are still clawing and the world keeps spinning like a carnival ride and that's it, we're going down, and then a hand catches mine. From out of nowhere a hand catches mine.

v

We carried our bones for days. Each night I wiped between my thighs and to my relief the paper came out clear.

v

The hand grips mine and won't let go. Not your father's.

Another hiker, his first day on the trail, heading south to north. *Can you move?* he asks.

v

The tide inched from shore, a thick retreating tongue. We scrambled three kilometres of boulders. I had visions of broken jaws, cracked femurs, and bashed-in skulls. You clung for dear life, but there was no reason to overreact. You were fine on that rocky shore. We were fine.

v

I writhe on my back with my eyes closed. I see only blood. Yours and mine.

v

That last night your dad and I cocooned like pupas in sleeping bags, our carcasses greasy and coated with fire smoke. We dared not touch or reach for each other.

v

He won't let go of my hand. The sky circles us. I'm dying. The leaves sway. Please don't let go.

v

By the seventh day, we were sour. Rose with the sun to a set of wooden ladders, one kilometre to the sky. It is true what they say. You have to hike the trail to experience the full capacity of its beauty. Photographs and stories just won't do.

ᐯ

Everything is broken. I'm sure of it. There is no way you
survived. It's over. The kind man says, *You're alright.*

ᐯ

The boat waits. In a few kilometres—a hot meal, a shower. A
bed.

ᐯ

I sit up. Welts on my hands. Balloon knee. Blood blooms a
butterfly on my shin, but nowhere else. We are still here.

ᐯ

There is nothing left to do but climb.

Q: Mom, will you still love me even when I kill you?

EVENTIDE

Grief
in the abdomen.
Shed clothes,
heat eternal.
Indigestion swoons.
Cervical canal
cauterized.

Night falls. Has fallen.
It is always this way—
darkness buries us.
Cloaked and bound.
Funnel eventide
down throat.

To birth from peace
is to un-live. Out of
body, I drift.
No one can
find me here.

Let it come
quickly.
                    Please.

Please.

YOUR FATHER

won't climb in the pool
with me. He will not put his
body on display.

BETTER BIRTHING THROUGH CHEMISTRY

Twilight sleep, popularized by Drs. Bernard Kronig and Karl
Gauss, combined morphine and scopolamine, a potentially toxic
cocktail that induced analgesia and amnesia, not anesthesia. The
distinction is crucial. Anesthesia provides complete pain relief and
unconsciousness. Analgesia offers partial pain relief. The added
amnesia meant that women felt pain but forgot about it—which
makes you wonder if anything is painful if there is no memory.
    —Randi Epstein, *Get Me Out: A History of Childbirth from the*
Garden of Eden to the Sperm Bank, 2010

Blindfolded and strapped,
gurneyed in my own shit,
the room dark for hours

or days, arms cast in
leather thongs—
Straitjacket Mommy.

Labour is for
the mentally ill.
Outside the hospital

pregnant women line up
for their injections. Scope blooms
with morphine, ticking time

bomb. Upper-class women
formed Twilight Sleep societies.
Quick prick and narcosis

complete. Rabbit hole
plummet into black forest.
Blue-tinted rooms,

eyes bound. Oil-soaked
cotton nests stuffed in ears
so I won't rouse

to my own screams. We go
a little crazy, don't we?
Alkaloid. Belladonna.

Deadly nightshade.
Each seductress straddles
hips and writhing belly. Best

not to fight.
Rectal injection. The burn
of babe in arms.

Emerge smooth vulva,
ingrown pubes. We wanted it then,
still do. Bell-shaped flower temptress.

We have our dignity. Sucklings
fresh and slick. Bliss
when we don't remember.

THE DISPLAY WINDOW

In the great green room
there is a noose and
a red blindfold and
a self-portrait of me
with a bag over my head.

DÄMMERSCHLAF

Twilight come
find me
in the bathtub
breathing drowning
writhing steam
vultures
my head there
but not really
there
everywhere
naked branded
flailing blanketed
suckled pig
peeled cored
alone alone
window ajar
sweat
can't stop
wetting
in piss vomit
oh god
my poor pussy

Don't believe
in survival
for all women
die this babe
is mine

or monster
every inch
of my fat
lacerates
iron sear
smoulder
between fetal
pulse
somehow sleep
the deep of pure
loathing
my satiety spun
stomach cistern
of bile

Twilight we are high
tripping off each
other's vibe
the way Dennis moves
his fingers
through my
hair perhaps
canal crushed
skull dissolved
bread crumbs
for birds
I forget your
cranium when I
come to
just wrap that
old doll

in a blanket
put it to my tit
that'll do

PAINLESS PARTURITION BY FRUIT DIET

If the embryo or fetus gradually consolidates, or increases in firmness and density by the accumulation of bony particles, will it not, at any given period of its existence, be more or less firm according to the bony matter which has been deposited? And is it not the mother's blood the source of this bony matter, since it builds, supports, and nourishes the fetus? And is not the mother's blood derived from her food and drink? And according to the proportion of bony matter existing in them, will not the fetus become more or less firm and resisting?

—M. L. Holbrook, *Parturition Without Pain*, 1896

Mr. Rowbotham had read that an embryo is mostly fluid, a gelatinous pulp that gradually hardens a skeletal core. One might crave cassowary anus and swamp eel to turn the birth canal a slippery mess. Stick to a diet of roasted apples, lemon juice, and rice boiled in milk for this gristly child to simply squish out, jelly carcass and limbs, then leap at the site of you, latch, bones hardening from your milk. I have never minded getting off easy. St. Paul's is just up the street. It looms like a castle or a post-apocalyptic erection. The buzz of fluorescent lights flicker as the strobe in my womb. Windows blink their eyes in wonderment. A softer, kinder baby was simply a question of diet. Less milk and spinach. More scurvy. Brilliant, sir. Such ingenuity. Imagine a soft cheese that slips between vaginal folds. An ethereal jam in the shape of my baby. Meditate on the soft spot until it becomes the entire head.

LAST STRAW

Straw suctioned
between chapped lips,
I suck with vigor.
Canines clench,
tongue pocked.
I submerge since
my diaper days.
Glide the length of
my childhood pool.
Mosquitoes swarm
thousands, hot summer
nights. I mermaid.
Tail waggles as bait.
I must be close.
The 12-hour mark
come and gone.
Proud morsel of lip
left. Cervical melt
down. Stick a finger
up me—I'm done.

ODE TO LUCY'S PELVIS

O wondrous one
her bipedal swag
terrestrial locomotion
partial appendages revealed
brain a soft sponge
size of an acorn still waiting
for that growth spurt
3.2 million years later.
Single pelvic bone
pubic arc
90 degrees too small
for a fourth trimester
to birth.
Her tailbone can't sway
like a flap door
for the dog to dash out.
Even the smallest skull would fuse
in her immature cavity.
I gulp air
like an asphyxiated pervert
lemon slice between my teeth.
Daylight descends over my lover's
greased brow
rivers through the blinds
rapids flooding hardwood.
The midwife squats in the corner
clipboard clutched to her chest.
Cheeks flushed

pressed to the wall.
The water tints from hours of use
blood, feces, vomit, urine.
Liquor amnii.
There's enough of my fluid
to douche a small village.
Between surges
the water's paralysis
breeds silence.
I curl fetal.
Calves throb
tendons convulse.
Pray for apoplexy.
The head is wedged
against my sacrum.
It must jimmy to the right
disengage.
My trunk wallows in swill.
I'd scrape knuckles against dirt
cripple spine, drag the razor
against my own gut
to have this nursling out.
It can grow dumb if need be.
Lucy, don't leave me like this.

CAROLYN BROKE MY WATER AND YOUR LUCK GUSHED OUT

(title to be sung to the tune of "Mama Had a Baby and Its Head Popped Off")

One of the most widespread of all the caul superstitions was that it would protect against drowning. Perhaps the most impressive support for this idea is a perfectly serious statement quoted in Notes and Queries regarding a baby born with a caul so effective "that when his mother tried to bathe him he sat on the surface of the water, and if forced down, came up again like a cork."
　　　　　—Thomas R. Forbes, *The Social History of the Caul*, 1953

Hours tick by,
contractions dull.
Cervix un-dilates.
Without pressure
from the head
much work
is undone.
I could have
prevented
your drowning
for life.
But it's okay.
You can buy
your own luck.
Raffles,
bargain bins,

flea markets.
Don your caul
like a cloak.
Run into
English Bay.
Flood the
ocean with
your breath.

TOKOPHOBICS UNITE

Posh Spice schedules her
surgeries around Beckham's
football tournaments.

ARMAMENTARIUM

Decapitators.
Symphysis knives, levers. Crude
hooks. The rib cage may

have malformed from the
corset, deformed from rickets.
L-shaped blunt grapnel.

Pincers. Oblong head
from the vectis, a fetus
insists on brute force.

Ingest laxatives.
Compress the skull, wrench tissue.
This will work in a

dystocic pinch. Make
sure you douche to drain toxins.
Babies who do not

come easily lack
a vital spirit. Pray to
the higher power.

The one with pure gall.
Speed is of the essence to
relieve this burden.

Cephalotribes: the
cranium perforators
of our frenetic

time. Then, Chamberlen
forceps, the granddaddy of
all obstetric tools.

Fenestrated blades,
their rounded edges. Word is
the Japanese use

an apparatus
of nets and whalebone. The French
stab the skull with a

poker, dismember
and purge. Premutilation,
midwife squirts holy

water up the birth
canal by syringe. We ooze
female. Laudable

pus. In utero
baptism before the babe's
noxious invasion.

Vermin can crawl up
the gaping hole. Crochet hook
is angled, gets lost

in the womb. Curettes
remove placenta. Inside
a fistula weeps.

A pessary is
required. Prepare yourself for
structural support.

In the end we must
master the way to wrench a
soul: quick like a milk

bunny. Even in
malignancy another
babe is born. Atoned.

I'VE MADE A TERRIBLE MISTAKE

I'm not like all those
other women. I will not
rise above myself.

TIME IS STILL (LINEAR)

My bowel—Iron
Maiden, tailbone swinging
on its hinges. Stuck in

this swamp, I bathe in
my juices. Water tepid
as stale coffee. The hardwood

floor is a sundial. Is it really
midafternoon? I have douched
enough, fermented

in amniotic piss. Fevered
flesh abrades air, the drug
of heat worn.

I am combustible.
Each breath
a limb shackled.

I should have passed
this cocoon hours ago.
Instead the baby

calcifies,
travels blind.
Lithos sarcophagus.

There should be an urge
to push. I feel nothing
but the shatter of bone,

the pectin pulp of belly.
A shudder along the abdominal
fault. Aftershock.

My thighs sputter.
I want my sister. Where
is my sister?

Her slumped shadow
in another prison
4,000 kilometres

south and three years
past. I teetered on
the rocking chair

in the next room,
watched edges of the sky
pink. There was nothing

I could do for her.
She was alone in her trough
as I am now.

Booze of light moves
through the shades. Time is still
linear. Fuck.

PATENT US 3216423 A

APPARATUS FOR FACILITATING THE BIRTH OF A CHILD BY
CENTRIFUGAL FORCE
AKA "THE BLONSKY"
NOVEMBER 9, 1965

*In the case of a woman who has a fully developed muscular system
and has had ample physical exertion all through the pregnancy,
as is common with all more primitive peoples, nature provides all
the necessary equipment and power to have a normal and quick
delivery. This is not the case, however, with more civilized women
who often do not have the opportunity to develop the muscles needed
in confinement.*

—George and Charlotte Blonsky, excerpt from their patent,
1965

The Blonskys had an extraordinary vision. An end to the trials
of pushing baby out.

The machine itself is made of heavy cast-iron aluminum
mounted on poured concrete and surrounded by a circular
fence. The patient is strapped horizontally along the radius
of the orbicular platform and spun like a merry-go-round,
maintaining the delicious force of up to seven Gs, thus creating
sufficient power to wrench aside constricting vaginal walls and
battle the friction of her uterus.

The physician acts simply as an amusement-ride operator, there
to employ the emergency brake only if the velocity of the child's
expulsion into the world fails to trigger the kill switch.

Baby is sucked out by centrifugal force and lands in a basket like Moses.

Aside from an irritating rope burn, the civilized woman is satisfied that she does not have to suffer in her birthing time.

The doctor is pleased. Everything according to schedule.

The Blonskys (George, a retired mining engineer, and his wife, Charlotte, a former medical student), a childless couple, celebrate with a dinner of Salisbury steak and mashed potatoes with a brown sauce.

FINALE

organ split
clit clipped
body wrenched
perineum stench
elasticized cone
stunted moan
meconium hair
oily skull tears
latched lips
ruptured shit

21 hours
and you didn't
come easy
but who does?

Q: Will you eat cake when I die? Like, on my birthday?

A: I'll never eat cake without you.

Q: Then what will you eat on my birthday?

A: I'll have pie.

Q: I like pie. With ice cream. Will you have a party for me when I die?

A: A party?

Q: Yeah. A party. Like the one you had for Granny when she died.

A: Yes. We'll have a celebration for you.

Q: When will you die?

A: Me? I...I don't know.

Q: Let's do it together.

PUSH

Everything is found in before
and after
it then *she*
the planet forced
through a rigid pelvis
everything explodes
our next one will
be adopted
eight cheerleaders
their pompoms held high
finger the cauliflower bulge
of scalp the shear
glass-cutting clit-splitting
of her crown
the planet of her erupts
into palms onto chest
her grandmother's face
cheeks plump nests
mouth a curved shell
clam-scented curls
screams sticky
swallows of sobs
chin creases fat rolls
speechlessness
galaxy shifts sacrum
hair slicked in waves
against a funnelled head.

My daughter.

ONCE SHE WAS BORN I WAS NEVER NOT AFRAID

Q-roo quakes
quavers

Q-tee-pie quaffs
quenches

Q-bert quantum
quintessential

Q-ball quarrels
querulous

Q-nami quashes
quells

My queasy heart
gutted.

THE CAT HAS THE STUNNED LOOK OF A MURDER WITNESS

Bloody rags. Feces
pool. Thin layer of vomit
in an ice cream pail.

STREPTOCOCCAL

*Physicians and medical students, who practiced obstetric exams
on cadavers, created a devastating cycle by going from the autopsy
slab—where decomposing bits of the body would stick under their
fingernails and in the creases of their skin—to the delivery table,
where they would perform internal exams to check for dilation or
descent. At no time in between did they wash their hands. They did
not know they should.*
                    —Tina Cassidy, *Birth: The Surprising History of How
                                          We Are Born,* 2006

Typically, fever struck within days of delivery,
followed by sharp pains that radiated
from the belly upward. Autopsies revealed
thick fetid pus suffocating the ovaries,
uterus, and abdomen. New mothers rotted away.
As if birth itself consumed them.

In 1836, a doctor blamed rotten breast milk
that leaked downward rather than out the nipples.
Dead mothers reeked the stench of rotten milk.
His unwashed hands a beacon of his prowess.
Others blamed constipation, new mother anxiety,
or cold air gushing into the open cervix.

Women were given laxatives, enemas
to drain toxins, chloride douches to cleanse
the birth canal. Barber surgeons favoured
bloodletting, encouraging leeches to suck out

the bad blood. Sometimes bugs crawled
up the vagina and were lost in the womb.

At the Boston Lying-In, doctors gave women
excessive doses of quinine to fight the fever
until their ears rang like a never-silent church bell.
The sudden cessation of pain, the fatal symptom.
Most died within a week of delivery, their putrid
remains lined along the rooftop to air.

SUPPLY AND DEMAND

Dennis goes back to work. I lactate.
The midwife listens to your tiny beat.
Jots down weight before and after feeds.
We eat dinner. You sleep in the bassinet.
The first and only time.

My spine is fused to pillows
piled in a throne. Udders leak and
mix with drool. The cat sleeps on your face
again. We trance in stupor.
I wet the bed with my tits.

No one wakes with us at night. My brain ossifies
by the flush of bedside lamp. My breasts are boulders.
I feed you at 11:46, 2:11, 4:18, and lose track.
Our bedroom is a dumpster. Used diapers, takeout
containers, granola bar wrappers. Breast pump.

Postpartum is the sewage system of a shrunken world.
You splay my chest. Starfish. Milk wastes under your weight.
My stomach is a flaccid blueprint of your past life.
Vacancy sings. It was a good harvest.
You pat my belly, the old stomping grounds.

HAIKUS FOR BABY BLUES

*Postpartum blues is a transient condition that 75–80% of mothers
could experience shortly after childbirth with a wide variety of
symptoms, which generally involve mood lability, tearfulness, and
some mild anxiety, and depressive symptoms.*
—Karandeep Kaur, *Puerperal Blues/Baby Blues/Postpartum Blues,*

2017

Don't worry, experts
coddle. You should be able
to just shake it off.

Like clockwork each night
our cramped apartment houses
a collective howl.

You arrived from my
erasure. I haunt our shared
bedroom. Leave me here.

I post a photo
of tiny fists to please my
antsy followers.

The baby blues is
not an illness. Think mood swings.
Hormones in transit.

My placenta left
a hole. Progesterone weeps
from me as you nurse.

My therapist says
fear is a bird that searches
for a place to land.

CEPHALOPELVIC

*An obstetric fistula is a hole between the vagina and rectum or
bladder that is caused by prolonged obstructed labour, leaving a
woman incontinent of urine or feces or both.*

—Fistula Foundation

Listen up and I'll tell you
how bedsides transform
into candlelit seance.
How they place sheets
over our putrid stink—
blooming transfixed
shadows. How we flicker
in and out of consciousness
not our own.
How we push too soon
with too much force,
crush and kill
the soft tissues of pelvis.
Prolonged labour—
cephalopelvic disproportion.
Uterus thrusts heads
into canals wedged
tight. Bladder, cervix,
vagina trapped under fierce
weight, immovable bony
plates. Blood supply cut,
uterine rupture,
hemorrhage, sepsis.

We live year after year
in ostracism and disgust.
Exude an ungodly
stench. Leak urine, feces.
Utter exhaustion
from days of labour
the least of our misery.
Women in rows upon
rows of beds. Misshapen
infant crowns or worse
crushed skulls, though some
held shape enough to
house a carnation
from a relative.
How a fetus asphyxiates
but we live
lying-in side by side.
Shitting and pissing the bed
as our nurslings would have.
Sometimes we are left
with the decaying seraph
inside. Our learned patience
as we wait. It macerates,
slips rotted from
our tubal slide.
Necrotic tissue separates
from the vesicovaginal
septum. Fistula.
She has a name.
We all did.

INVESTMENT

Time to move on from birth.
There is more to consider
than how fetuses are expelled.
The dichotomy of self is infinite.
One then two then two again,
squalling infant
dependent on host.
I am collateral. The embryo
grows into a star
with limbs of its own,
mouth and anus.
If anything happens to that sweet
starfruit, I am finished.
I've been conditioned
through shared hormones, cells,
genetic imperatives
to believe you are the most intoxicating being
on this planet.
For that reason alone
I should not eat you.
I drool over thigh ripples,
quivering mounds of gelatin.
You are positively hoggish.
A nursing mother needs calories.
I need more than I ever have.
Is this a love poem
or a poem of grief?
When we make something
we lose.

THE MOTHER BECOMES THE BACKGROUND AGAINST WHICH THE BABY LIVES

Bounce you in the coffee shop.
Jog you along the seawall.
Oh, for Christ's sake, don't drop
the cellphone on your face!
Jiggle you at dim sum.
Turn you over
to smell your bum.
Change you in the night,
you're a backed-up sewer pipe—
pray you won't roll off
as I turn to grab the wipes.
Fasten you against my chest.
Dance you into high-pitched shrieks.
Spill you out of the carrier,
zigzagged face, zipper creased.
Hold you against my stomach,
imagine how you once fit.
Feed you my nipple to shut you up
when I need to take a shit.
Shine your face with baby soap.
Shampoo your inky swoops of hair.
Swim you in the bath
as legs sprocket without care.
Swaddle you so your arms won't flail
and smack you hard in slumber.
Poke until you take deep breaths,

sigh them out and shudder.
Carry you in the dead of sleep.
Nurse you drunk and drooling.
Cycle your legs to force the gas out,
rancid feces pooling.
Chew those rolls along your thighs—
luscious, delectable, yum.
Exhaust you with my antics.
Eat you with my love.

WE'LL NEVER BE ALONE AGAIN

I mount Dennis, hiss
She's down, let's go, so we do,
each with our ears cocked.

BREASTFEEDING IN MY PARENTS'
BASEMENT AT 3 A.M.

Upstairs Granny with her walker
switches *lights on lights on*. Juggernaut.
She's the house stalker.

I scarf yesterday's maki, scroll Gawker.
My sleeping baby within earshot
stirs as Granny with her walker

zombies the floor, a boat rocker.
Dimmers plunge like slide whistles. Fraught,
she's the house stalker.

In sweat-soaked sheets, I mock her.
Night thickens. Bloated with arousal, my hand drops
down and Granny's squeaking walker

shocks my pink squid awake. My little squawker's
all tentacles and squinty eyes from the cot.
Upstairs, Granny's predator stalks her.

Decay inherits itself, sweet talker.
Bedside leftovers rot.
Upstairs, Granny with her walker
is the house matriarch, my stalker.

ONE FUCK OF A YEAR

Grandma Kim, your dad's adopted mom,
is dying. She gave you the giraffe stuffy

that plays soft African drums and you clutch
one of its legs while you dream.

She came to visit days before your first birthday.
Her wife pushed her in a wheelchair,

leg fractured, full of cancer.
Thirty years ago, your biological grandmother

drove from Victoria to Winnipeg with ash
in her lungs, a hacking cough

that ended the trip in hospital.
She never left.

Dennis was 19. Blew his inheritance
on motorcycles and trucks.

Blood money, he called it.
We went to the aquarium and

you watched the belugas from
Grandma Kim's lap. She whispered

in your ear, her vocal cords
clipped like cut wires.

I could be sad. I am sad. But it also seems
par for the course that you must

learn to lose her
before you even know her.

I have lost no one. My mother
may have lost her mind

but there's been no official diagnosis yet.
Her body is here, though it paces

aimlessly through the house.
She dollops margarine instead

of butter on my Granny's potatoes
who doesn't complain but gives thanks

to my mother over and over
for such a magnificent dinner.

Even though Granny is demented,
I see our resemblance.

It's worrisome. The fridge is tied up in knots
from her incessant rummaging.

But your grandma Kim is kind.
She held your fat slippery body

in the pool last summer
while you kicked and kicked

those bratwurst legs,
swollen with my milk.

Now, in the middle of writing this,
there is more news.

Grandma Kim has had a stroke.
She's at Health Sciences in Winnipeg.

I was trying to order a stuffed monkey
for her from the gift shop when I heard.

They found two shadows on her brain.
Things are happening faster

than I can record them.
My mother can't shake her paranoia.

There's never enough food for the party;
the hospital she stayed in during her breakdown

is charging her with fraud;
where's that neurology team

and why couldn't they find anything
on the CT scan? And somewhere,

in another hospital, my best friend's
father has a brain biopsy.

The next months will be his shitty diapers
and my friend losing her mind with grief.

I will catch a glimpse
of his 61-year-old penis

during a sponge bath, tell my friend
and we will giggle ourselves

to tears. My mom will get better.
She will recover and get her retirement.

My friend's dad will move
into hospice and hallucinate

chairs on the ceiling, talk about
the resurrection, update his Facebook status

with gibberish. He will die.
I will miss his funeral and regret it.

2014, you are one fuck of a year.
But we don't know all of this yet.

All we know is Grandma Kim's lungs
are bleeding. She's on morphine.

She's discontinued treatment.
It will be any day now.

You have finally fallen asleep.
Sick with a nose like a faucet,

frothing bubbles on your upper lip.
Raspy shallow breaths.

In the night your body writhes,
possessed. I give you my breast.

Your mucus covers my nipple.
The year unfolds. Hold on.

A: C'mon, Q, let's go down to English Bay.

FLOOD THE OCEAN WITH
YOUR BREATH

I.

I come first. Heady
with drink, sunstroke.

Pure hedonist,
I'll ravage.

I get what I want.
We swoon in afternoon sweat.

Binge ourselves. He mimics
his drunk spunk.

The water inside me
a medium.

2.

Belly grows taut
first try.

In nematodes,
sperm cells crawl

rather than swim
toward the her

cell. Spawn
in darkness.

Amnion fills with fluid.
I am your cavity.

3.

I will claw his
fucking eyes out.

All fours, amoeboid,
unsightly. I beg

to have you yanked out
quick as a loose tooth.

Leave me sterile,
I don't care.

Instead, waters pierced.
I pickle.

4.

My debut into motherhood
polycephalic

as you pause, half-in,
half-out of me.

Born but not
born. Ethereal

between bloody
thighs. Hard push.

You dredge up
along my shore.

5.

I shower off blood
and bravery,

but who was brave here?
I prayed for a surgeon's

salient hands and
weaponry. My organs

slide into place.
Your raw head rests

on my belly.
Waterbed.

6.

Chafed from confectionary
milk and sweat,

I want
for everything.

Howl
from the bedroom

suspends
in chronology.

Night after night I plunge,
subaqueous.

7.

For days your head
smells like me.

I transform from
hero to her.

Consume my afterbirth
to ward off voices,

balm for baby blues.
Captivity leaves us

heartsick,
waterlogged.

8.

Sweet Roo,
how do I find you?

How do I rid myself
of you, sweetmeat?

Your father by himself
in the other room.

Is he sorry?
Am I? An ocean

between and your
life raft is me.

Q: Mom, I have to tell you something. It's really important.

A: What's that, bug?

Q: I love you sizzle hearts and that means never stop.

ANSWERS

It has been almost a year
and now I sit
in a coffee shop
read *Our Andromeda*
for the third time.
In the moment of peril
the last heat of push
some cry for God
some for love.
We are taught
that God *is* love and
I can believe that, I don't
care either way.
I named you.
My love. My love.
Those final five seconds
a noose slipped
around memory.
I siphoned the last
drops of viable water
to quench
an insatiable thirst.
Some call out *God*
during sex
or birth or even
in death but I said
Love. Love
with every force
of my being.

NOTES AND ACKNOWLEDGEMENTS

Lines were borrowed for "Questions" from various texts by
Brenda Shaughnessy, Rachel Rose, Anne Sexton, Quintana
Roo Dunne, William Wordsworth, John F. Kennedy, and Joan
Didion. Much gratitude to the original authors.

"The waves, unless there is water, are calm, roll a body gently"
in "Not Trying" is a variation on a line from Lidia Yuknavitch's
memoir, *The Chronology of Water.*

"What to Expect When You're Expecting (100 Years Ago)" and
"Hygiene of Antenatal Life" contain text from J. H. Kellogg's
*Ladies' Guide in Health and Disease: Girlhood, Maidenhood,
Wifehood, Motherhood.*

"The Display Window" draws inspiration from the children's
book *Goodnight Moon* by Margaret Wise Brown.

"Once She Was Born I Was Never Not Afraid" is a line from
Joan Didion's memoir, *Blue Nights.*

"Streptococcal" contains text from Randi Epstein's book *Get Me
Out: A History of Childbirth.*

"You pat my belly, the old stomping grounds" in "Supply and
Demand" is a line from Susan Holbrook's poem "Nursery."

"The Mother Becomes the Background against Which
the Baby Lives" is a line from Sarah Manguso's memoir,
Ongoingness: The End of a Diary.

Earlier drafts of these poems were published in various Canadian literary magazines. A suite of poems from this book, under the title "A Short History of Childbirth in North America," won *SubTerrain*'s 15th Annual Lush Triumphant Poetry Contest. An earlier version of "Gestational Fall" won the 2015 Great Blue Heron Poetry Award and was published as a chapbook by above/ground press. Thank you to the editors and judges who acknowledged these poems.

This book would not have been possible without generous financial assistance from the BC Arts Council and the Canada Council for the Arts.

Ω

My thanks and love to:

Everyone at Book*hug, especially Jay MillAr and Hazel Millar. To say I feel lucky to publish with you is an understatement. Special thanks to Kate Hargreaves for your gorgeous cover design and Stuart Ross for copy editing.

Brecken Hancock, editor and dear friend. These poems were eagerly awaiting your eyes and heart to propel them into their best selves.

Alex Leslie, PHOEM editor extraordinaire. My soup is your soup.

Elee Kraljii Gardiner, for your thoughts and friendship.

Marianne Apostolides, for your words.

My family, immediate and extended, especially my mom, Margaret Gruber. And to my Granny, Barbara Lucille Creighton. I hope you're having a cocktail with Granddad right now.

Domini Meyer and Ebony Paquet, the first babies I witnessed being born. How are you both almost adults?

All the Q-sitters over the years. Especially Richard Hill and Bev Koski, for loving my girls as your own.

Carolyn Saunders, Andrea Mattenley, Jessica Austin, and Megan Taylor, for holding space.

My lifelines in motherhood: Taran Meyer, Jennifer Floyd, Brecken Hancock, Edith Gruber, Taunya Staffen, Anne-Marie Jamin, Allison Cammer, Anita McCartney, Morgan Sather, Emma Lind, and Amanda Casile.

Matthew Trafford and Linda Besner: sweetest companions during the earliest of drafts.

Dennis Hill. Your role in this book is pretty obvious. Xoxo.

Tamsin. I was pregnant with you when I was working on the first draft of this book, so we basically wrote it together. You're the most hilarious and wackiest kid I have ever known. Don't ever change.

Quintana Roo. I was sure when I had you my writing career was over. Did you ever prove me wrong. Sizzle hearts, my love, forever.

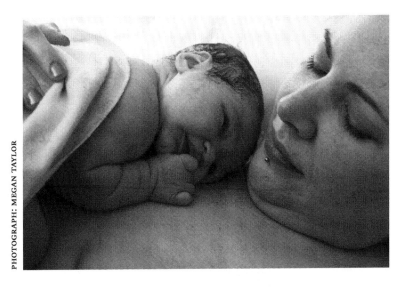

PHOTOGRAPH: MEGAN TAYLOR

ADRIENNE GRUBER is the author of two books of poetry, *Buoyancy Control* (Book*hug) and *This is the Nightmare* (Thistledown Press), and five chapbooks. She won *The Antigonish Review*'s Great Blue Heron poetry contest in 2015, *SubTerrain*'s Lush Triumphant poetry contest in 2017 and has been shortlisted for the CBC Literary Awards, *ARC*'s Poem of the Year contest, *Descant*'s Winston Collins Best Canadian Poem contest and *Matrix Magazine*'s Lit POP poetry contest. In 2012, her chapbook, *Mimic* was awarded the bpNichol Chapbook Award. Originally from Saskatoon, Adrienne lives in Vancouver with her partner and two daughters. *Q & A* is her third book.

COLOPHON

Manufactured as the first edition of
Q & A in the spring of 2019
by Book*hug Press.

Edited for the press by Brecken Hancock
Copy edited by Stuart Ross
Type + design by Kate Hargreaves